The International Food Fair!

by Jana Martin
illustrations by Joe Bucco

Scott Foresman
is an imprint of

Glenview, Illinois • Boston, Massachusetts • Chandler, Arizona
Upper Saddle River, New Jersey

ISBN 13: 978-0-328-50841-9
ISBN 10:   0-328-50841-1

Who was supposed to make dinner at the Kyles' house tonight?

"Isn't it your turn?" Mrs. Kyle said to Mr. Kyle.

"I thought it was your turn," Mr. Kyle said to Mrs. Kyle. "What should we do?"

Mr. and Mrs. Kyle taught at the local college. Their children, Amy, Allie, and Danny loved to visit the college. They liked the fact that the students came from around the world.

"Hey," Mr. Kyle said. "Let's not eat alone. Tonight is the college's International Food Fair. We can buy food from other countries!"

The food fair took up half of the gym! There were tables and flags. Students and teachers offered food from their homes. There were people from Mexico, Thailand, France, Kenya, and many other countries.

"Hello Mr. and Mrs. Kyle!" said a girl at the Chinese food table. "These must be your children."

"These are our daughters, Amy and Allie," Mrs. Kyle said. "And this is our son, Danny. He is our youngest."

"What are you serving?" asked Mr. Kyle.

"*Dim sum*," said the girl. "The words mean 'touch the heart,' but it really just means 'snack.' Many dishes are a part of dim sum, like the spring roll. It's a thin pancake that is rolled around pork and vegetables, then fried."

"Delicious!" said Danny, taking two.

"Welcome to a tiny slice of Ghana," said the boys at another table.

"Ghana's in West Africa," Amy said. "I learned that in school. What's the mushy stuff?"

The boys laughed. "That is mashed yam, called *fufu*. It's like bread to us."

Next, the Kyles decided to try food
from France. The French girl said,
"Try some *crepes*. They are very thin
pancakes."

She poured batter on a hot pan, then
added cheese. "Who wants a bite?"
she asked, folding the cooked crepe.
Everyone did!

The Kyles had their dinner. Now it was time for dessert.

Mr. Kyle laughed as Danny eyed the table with food from Italy. "Would you like a cannoli?" Mr. Kyle asked. "It's stuffed with sweet cheese and chocolate chips."

"Yummy!" said Amy, Allie, and Danny, together.

"Hey," Amy said. "Know what? That was the best dinner ever."

"I'm glad we forgot whose turn it was to cook!" said Mrs. Kyle. "It was fun to eat dinner around the world!"

A World of Dough

The pancakes that wrapped the Chinese spring rolls would have been made from rice. The pancakes known as French crepes would have been made from wheat. If you were to go to Mexico, you would find something that looks like a pancake that is made from corn—a tortilla.

Different countries use different grains to make their dough, but the foods often end up with similar shapes. This is because people worldwide have similar needs. Think about foods you know that are easy to cook or easy to carry.

Many countries have some kind of pancake. In the United States, pancakes usually come with butter and syrup.

12